Contents

1. Introduction 1
2. How to use this resource? 2
3. Use your hands (b, d, p, g, s, z) 3
4. What are Bbs and Dds doing? 11
5. Does it fit in a box? (b, d) 13
6. What goes first? (b, d, p, q) 15
7. Use your whole body (b, d, p, q, s, z) 20
8. Five and six do not mix! (all digits) 24
9. Which way is 3? 26
10. Which way are 6 and 9? 27
11. Word and sentence lists 30
12. Key to activities 32

1. Introduction

A warm welcome as you're opening this resource. You're most likely to be a teaching professional or parent/carer, who is concerned about your pupil's/child's letter and digit reversals. It is not unusual for primary school children to continue confusing graphic shapes beyond Key Stage 1 despite normal vision, adequate pen control, good spatial awareness, and often good overall literacy and numeracy skills. The majority of children 'grow out' of the reversing stage at some point during Key Stage 2. Even children with dyslexia and dysgraphia, who take longer to learn to write and spell, normally make the reversals breakthrough before entering secondary school, with only occasional b/d reversals showing up in their scripts.

So why this workbook? It's written for younger children who might feel so confused and discouraged that they avoid writing, or write very little, despite having great imaginations. They start doubting their ability to simply 'know' the correct way when writing b/d, p/q, p/g, 9/g, 6/9, s/z, 5/S, S/3, etc. Most teachers and parents are very good at playing down the reversals and encouraging the child to have another go. They say, "It's fine, it's still good writing. I love what you've written here." Yet, after so many attempts and after so many teacher corrections on the page, the child begins to think, "This writing game might not be for me after all". Those with dyslexia will have additional phonological difficulties to manage alongside poor memory for graphic shapes.

Although this resource is a practical workbook, it doesn't show correct starting points for writing letters and digits. There are many excellent Early Years and Key Stage 1 resources that demonstrate how to teach letter and digit formation - parents will recognise them by lined pages with dots and arrows within large-print characters showing the exact direction in which the pencil should follow. These resources work very well for most children in the classroom: "Start with an l stroke when writing b, and a c stroke for d". The child's fingers soon 'know' what to do.

But not all pupils learn the rules of graphic directionality that way. This workbook is for children who can trace well at speed, thus appear to have developed adequate motor memory in their fingers, yet struggle to remember 'which way' to write the letter or digit. It is very likely that they will be ready to integrate this type of linear visual-spatial information at a later time. For now, they have no real-life representation, or model, of a handful of graphic shapes in their brains, and this, in turn, can affect their confidence in writing independently.

This workbook aims to bring fun back into writing by demonstrating how to stop the reversal confusion. It offers practical and long-term 'tricks' that will trigger the child's memory at the right moment. The resource adopts a complementary approach to traditional letter formation teaching to bridge the gap between children who are proficient graphic writers and those whose brains make different sense of graphic information. Many children with dyslexia and dysgraphia will particularly benefit from completing the workbook.

2. How to use this resource

1. The child doesn't need to work through the entire book. Choose sections that are relevant to their needs.

2. Younger children (aged 4-6) will most likely need assistance when working with the resource, although older ones will no doubt choose to work independently, showing their practised strategies and completed activities to teachers and parents. It is recommended that section 7 (Use your whole body) is attempted with the help of an older helper or adult. Pages 30-31 contain word and sentence lists for teachers and parents to help the child consolidate their newly acquired letter writing skills.

3. There are more than one method to help distinguish between b/d/p and s/z in this workbook. Introduce the child to only one method at a time, evaluate the child's progress, and decide whether there is a need to move on to the next one. Some children are more practical than visual - the 'Use your hands' strategy might be sufficient for them. Other children might enjoy more visual strategies in sections 4, 5 and 6. In my experience, section 7 (Use your whole body) works well with children who need to 'experience' concepts in a multi-sensory manner. Pay attention to the child's initial response to a particular method. It will guide you along.

4. You can mix and match strategies. Some children don't confuse b/d as much but struggle with p/9. Find relevant sections for p and 9 confusions, and combine them into a modified strategy for the child, for example using the hands method for p ('pig' or 'pug') and the caterpillar or chair method for 9. Even if the child only remembers one method, they will know the other character must be the opposite shape.

5. Some activities can be completed independently of the section the child is currently working through. For example, Activity 7 can be attempted after completing the 'Use your hands' section. Flick through the book to decide which activities appear to be suitable to the child's current progress. Don't forget to look at pages 30-31.

6. Be involved as much as you can. Remind the child of the strategies as often as possible in everyday situations so they can be 'over-learned'. Here are some examples:
"Did you enjoy meeting Ben at Auntie Jo's? How do we write a b, again? Bat before what, Freddie, when you're writing a b? And what did we say for a d? What before what, again? Well done. You knew that straight away this time. I'm really proud of you."
"It's almost 6 o'clock. What can six do that nine can't? That's right. Six sits in a chair without falling off."
"Freddie, did you say you wanted to show Nan how to make the words 'bed', 'pug', and 'scary zombie' on your hands?"

7. Although this resource focuses on the most common letter and digit reversals, some of its multi-sensory, practical ideas can be modified to apply to less common reversals, e.g. n/u, m/w, n/m, etc. Activity 13 might be a good starting point for a spot of inspiration.

I hope you and your child/children will have as much fun working with this resource as I did putting it together with the help of primary school-age children I had the enormous pleasure to engage with as part of my dyslexia assessment and support work.

Lidia Stanton

lidia.stanton@icloud.com   in https://uk.linkedin.com/in/lidiastanton   f https://facebook.com/dyslexiaideas

ISBN: 1548579122
ISBN-13: 978-1548579128

3. Use your hands

b and d

Ben is fast asleep in his bed.
We can make the word 'bed' using our hands.
But without Ben. We'll leave him in his bed.

Can you see how your fingers and thumbs are making the two letters?

Have you got it? Good work.

Activity 1

What's missing: a **b** or **d** stroke next to the pictures?
The first two letters have been completed for you.
Use your hands to check
how to write **b** and **d**.

Make O into b or d.

3

p and g

Make the word 'bed' on your fingers.
Very good!

Now turn both hands upside down.
And we have the word 'pig'.

bed

pig

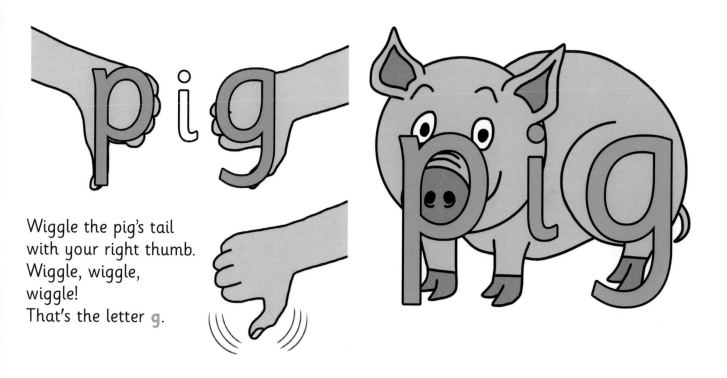

Wiggle the pig's tail
with your right thumb.
Wiggle, wiggle,
wiggle!
That's the letter g.

If you prefer, we can make the word 'pug' instead of 'pig'.

Now help the pug wag its tail.
Swish, swash! Swish, swash!

Did you wiggle your right
thumb?

Good work.

Look who's happy now!

Activity 2

What's missing: a **p** or **g** stroke next to the pictures?
The first two letters have been completed for you.
Use your hands to check how to write **p** and **g**.

Make o into p or g.

6

Activity 3

Read the clues and write the missing words. Every stepping line is one letter. Use your hands to check how to write **b**/**d**/**p**/**g**.

_ _ _
not good

_ _
not down

_ _ _
on a washing line

_ _ _
not hot

_ _ _ _
small horse

_ _
green traffic light

_ _ _
you sleep in it

_ _ _
colour of a pig

_ _ _
not small

_ _ _
space between teeth

_ _ _ _
where money comes from

_ _ _
not a cat

_ _ _
not a girl

_ _ _ _
better than silver

_ _ _ _
postman with a cat called Jess

_ _ _
use it to hit a cricket ball

_ _ _ _
house for farm animals

_ _ _
put rubbish in it

_ _ _
not a mum

_ _ _ _
person with no hair

_ _ _
do it with a spade

_ _ _
hot cross cake

_ _ _ _
goes with a wall socket

_ _ _
insect

_ _ _
red double decker

_ _ _ _
teeth twice a day

_ _ _
keeps baby's top clean

_ _ _
buzzing insect

_ _ _
smallest coin

_ _ _
famous Peppa

_ _ _
not a pencil

_ _ _ _ _
long yellow fruit

_ _ _
baby flower

_ _ _
your own animal

_ _ _ _ _
delivers letters

7

s and z

Is this meant to be a **s**cary **z**ombie, Illustrator?
No one is scared. And what about his googly eyes?
They make him look like a **s**illy **z**ombie.

We can make the zombie's eyes with our fingers.

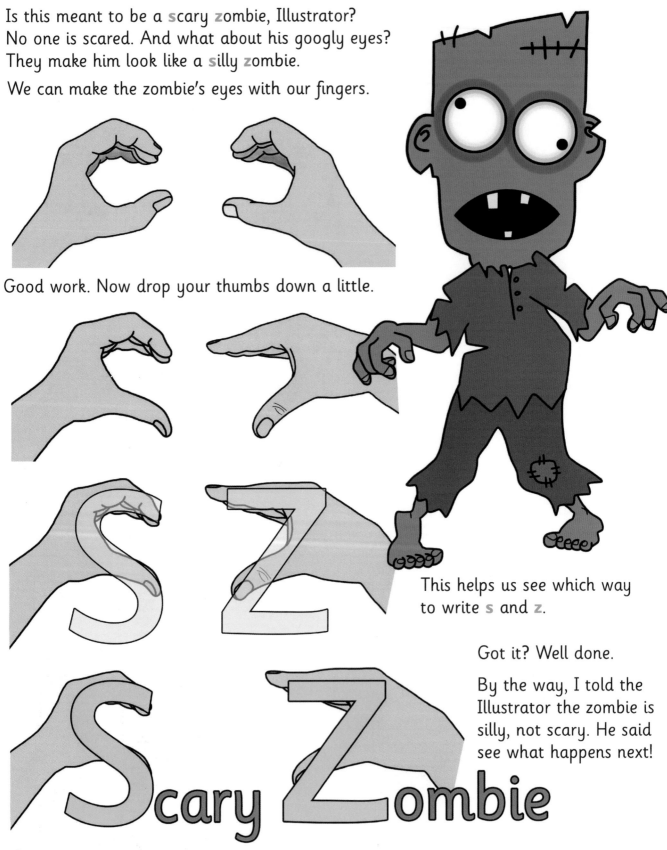

Good work. Now drop your thumbs down a little.

This helps us see which way to write **s** and **z**.

Got it? Well done.

By the way, I told the Illustrator the zombie is silly, not scary. He said see what happens next!

Scary **Z**ombie

Now drop your hands down as if they were **really** heavy.

Did you hear that terrible noise?

The **s**cary **z**ombie's arms have dropped off!

But he hasn't noticed. He's too sleepy, yawwwwning away...

We were right all along. He's not scary at all. Just a **s**leepy **z**ombie...

Can you make '**s**leepy **z**ombie' on your hands?

Activity 4

Write **s** or **z** in the bubbles next to the pictures. The first two have been completed for you. Use your hands to check the shapes of **s** and **z**.

Activity 5

Someone is not happy with their friend. But why? Write **s** or **z** in the missing gaps in the email to find out.
Use your hands to check the shapes of the two letters.

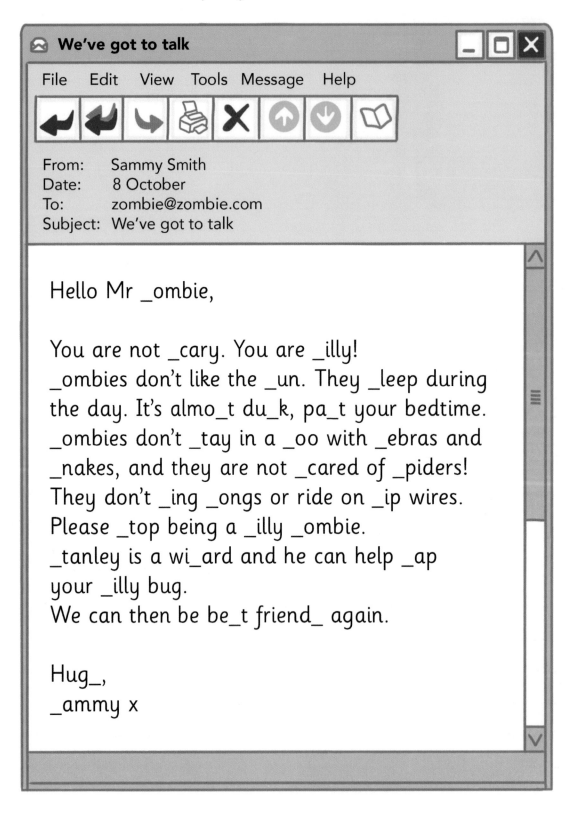

We've got to talk

File   Edit   View   Tools   Message   Help

From: Sammy Smith
Date: 8 October
To: zombie@zombie.com
Subject: We've got to talk

Hello Mr _ombie,

You are not _cary. You are _illy!
_ombies don't like the _un. They _leep during
the day. It's almo_t du_k, pa_t your bedtime.
_ombies don't _tay in a _oo with _ebras and
_nakes, and they are not _cared of _piders!
They don't _ing _ongs or ride on _ip wires.
Please _top being a _illy _ombie.
_tanley is a wi_ard and he can help _ap
your _illy bug.
We can then be be_t friend_ again.

Hug_,
_ammy x

4. What are Bbs and Dds doing?

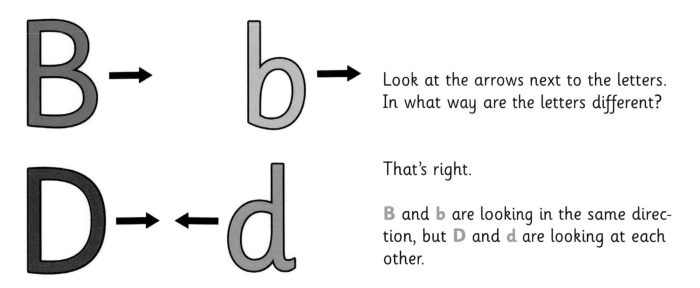

Look at the arrows next to the letters. In what way are the letters different?

That's right.

B and b are looking in the same direction, but D and d are looking at each other.

This is because:

Bbs like to walk	and	**Dd**s like to talk
Best **b**uddies like to walk	and	**D**a**d**s like to talk

Activity 6

My **b**est **b**uddy (best friend) is called

....

Draw two heads on top of **B** and **b**:
one for you, one for your buddy.

Make sure you're walking in the same
direction!

Now draw two heads for talking **D**a**d**s.

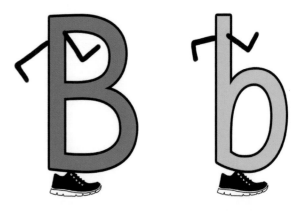

What do you think **D**a**d**s are talking
about? Choose one topic:

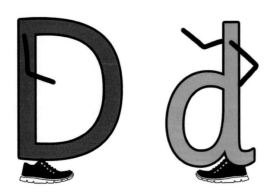

dancing	dentists	dinners
dragons	disco	desserts
dreams	driving	doctors
detectives	dogs	drumming
dolphins	diamonds	deer
diet	diving	dolls	ducks
donkeys	doors	drawing

Now finish the script. Make sure the conversation is very silly!

Dad 1: You won't believe what I've heard about ....

Dad 2: ....

Dad 1: ....

Dad 2: ....

Dad 1: ....

Dad 2: ....

Dad 1: ....

5. Does it fit in a box?

What will happen if we try to fit **b** and **d** in a box?

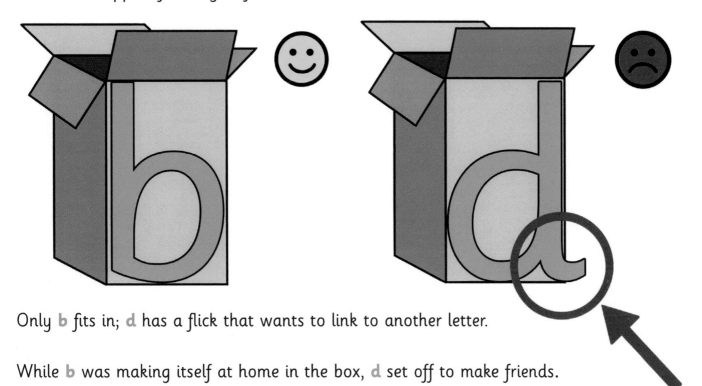

Only **b** fits in; **d** has a flick that wants to link to another letter.

While **b** was making itself at home in the box, **d** set off to make friends.

As it tried to quietly fit through our door, its flick knocked very loudly.
'Can I help you?', asked **Dad**.
'I'm a letter', answered **d**.
'The only letters we are waiting for are with the post-man', **Dad** looked puzzled.
'I also need a letter, or letters. My flick has no one to link to', explained **d**.
At that moment, **ice** was passing by and overheard **d**.
'Just as well', said **ice**. 'I'm melting away in this sun!'

You know what happened next, don't you?

And that's the story of how **d**'s flick changed **ice** into **dice**, making friends with children who loved board games.

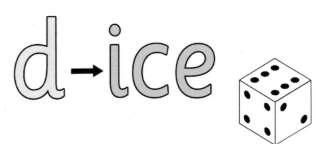

While **b** stayed in the box, **d** explored the alphabet making more and more words, and more and more friends. What a friendly letter.

13

Activity 7

What's missing: a **b** or **d** stroke next to the pictures? The first two letters have been completed for you. Remember **b** fits into a box and **d** has a flick that wants to link to another letter.

Make o into b or d.

6. What goes first?

Some pictures are in the shape of tricky letters. Remember the picture and you'll know the letter. Now, what goes first?

Cricket is a game of bat and ball, not the other way round. Have your bat ready before the ball hits it.

 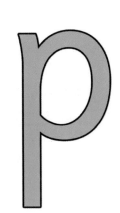

bat before ball

A drummer sets up his drum before he reaches for his drumsticks.

drum before drumstick

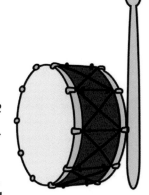 

You need a pin to pop things.

pin before pop

The queen is wearing a round collar.

queen before collar

Activity 8

Can you remember the four pictures on the page before? What did they tell us?

b.................................... before ....

d.................................... before ....

p.................................... before ....

q.................................... before ....

Now draw the pictures in the boxes below to help you remember what goes first.

b	d
p	q

Have you noticed that when you write q, the next letter is always u. Do you know why? Because the queen always carries an umbrella with her - just in case it rains on her magnificent crown and gown.

In this way, q and u are always together.

Not only in the word 'queen' but in all words with q that you will write at school.

We can glue the letters together by linking the stroke in q to u.

queen

queen + umbrella

The two letters now look like one long letter shape qu.

Activity 9

Copy the words below. Connect q to u with a long stroke so they look like qu. This will help you remember: when you write q, always follow it with u.

quiz .... **qu**eue ....

quack .... **qu**arry ....

question .... **qu**een ....

quiet .... **qu**ick ....

Activity 10

Complete the letter shapes next to the pictures by drawing strokes.

Make o into b, d, p, g or q.

19

7. Use your whole body

It looks like Lucy is exercising. She has learned how to write **b**, **d**, **p**, **q**, **s** and **z** by becoming the tricky letters while lying on the floor. We can do that, too. You'll need a helper to be with you during this activity.

Find an empty and safe space on the floor, and lie down. Put a cushion, or rolled up blanket, at your feet and feel it with your toes. Pretend the cushion is the writing line that words sit on.

You're now a big letter on a big line.

Close your eyes and imagine what you look like from above. Let your mind's eye 'see' the letter's curves, lines and strokes.

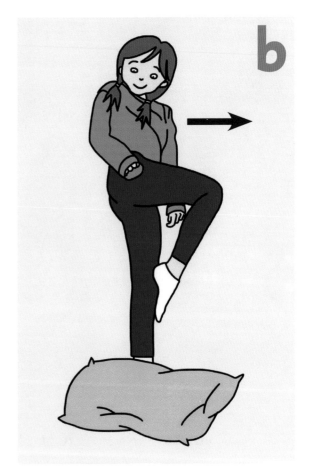

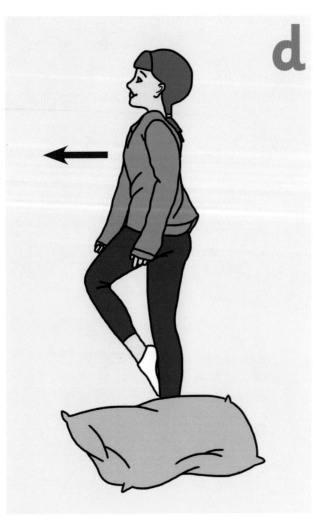

Think of as many words that start with the letter as you can. Say them out loud while imagining you **are** the first letter in each word.

b and d

You're lying on your side when making these letters. If you're a **b**, you can see the rest of the word spreading on the floor in front of you. It's so easy it's a **b**reeze.

If you're a **d**, it's really hard to turn your head all the way to see the whole word. It's **d**ifficult for a **d** to see the rest of the word. You're looking away from the word.

p

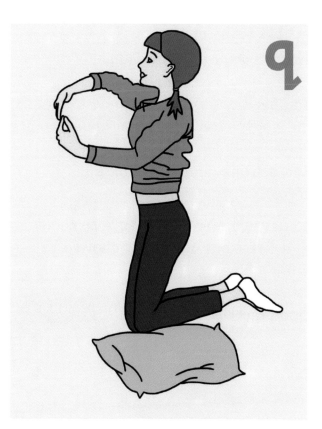

q

Now make the letters p, q, s and z. What does it feel like to be each of them in turn? Can you see the whole word you're thinking of when you have become q and z? Why?

s

z

Activity 11

This is Lucy's favourite game.

You need two or more people to play it. Roll a dice, then check the box for which letter shape you have to make on the floor.

You get one point when an adult has checked that your letter shape is correct.

To get two points, you have to come up with a word that starts with that letter but you're not allowed to use the same word more than once in the game.

Good luck!

1........**b**

2........**d**

3........**p**

4........**q**

5........**s**

6........**z**

Activity 12

Do you know anyone who can say the alphabet without singing the alphabet song?

Me neither. Even if they say they can, I wouldn't be so sure. I reckon they are singing it quietly in their heads.

Why not sing along with me now? Write the missing letters of the alphabet in the blue box.

a _ c _

e _ _

h i _ _

l _ _ o _

_ r _

t _ _

_ x

_ _

Activity 13

If you liked making letters with your whole body, you'll love making them with play-dough, beads, Lego blocks or similar building bricks, sticks, leaves, straws, pipe cleaners, pasta shapes, popsicle sticks, raisins, pebbles, and other things you can find at home and in the garden.

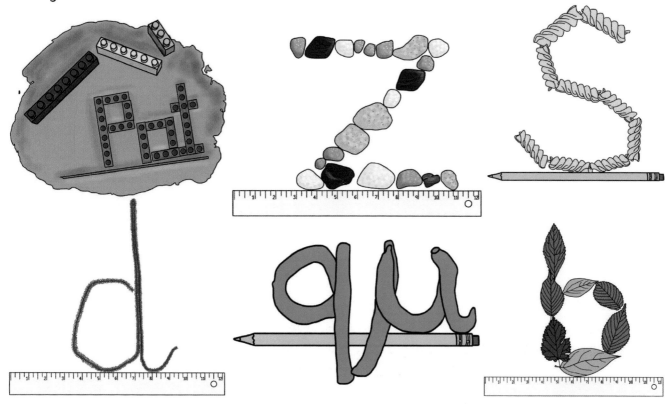

Always have a line on which your letters can sit. You can draw a line on paper or use a ruler or pencil as your pretend line.
Without a line, your letter will think it's in space and will keep changing directions because you can do that in space.
Just look what happened to **b**.

23

8. Five and six do not mix!

What a fun looking caterpillar.
Lots of happy faces. But what's that?
Two digits are doing something silly...

5 and 6 are looking in the opposite direction
and are not following 0.

They can't see their leader.
Oh, dear.

Five and six do not mix!

Activity 14

Draw faces (eyes and mouth) in the digits below to show which way they are looking.
Colour them in green if they are following 0, or red if they are going in the opposite direction.

3 4 2 6 7 1 5

9 5 3 4 2 6 8

6	2	3	1	7	8	3
4	9	5	6	2	9	5

Now check that only **5** and **6** are coloured in red because **five and six do not mix**.

Next time you're not sure which way to write a digit, think if they are following 0 or not.

Activity 15

We all have important numbers: Tell me about yours.

I am ___ years old.

At school, I am in year ___.

My house or flat number is ___.

My favourite number is ___.

I have ___ sibling(s) (brothers and sisters).

I was born in the year _____.

Today's date is ___/___/_____.

I sometimes find it hard to write the number(s) ____ and ____.

I have ___ pet(s).

9. Which way is 3?

Find 3 on the caterpillar.

3 is following 0. Let's find its face. Is it looking the same way as 0? Yes, it is.

Two 3s make a butterfly. But which is 3: blue or red?

Let's count all wings, small and big.

The third wing is number 3. It tells us how to write 3.

And here it is. The right way round.

10. Which way are 6 and 9?

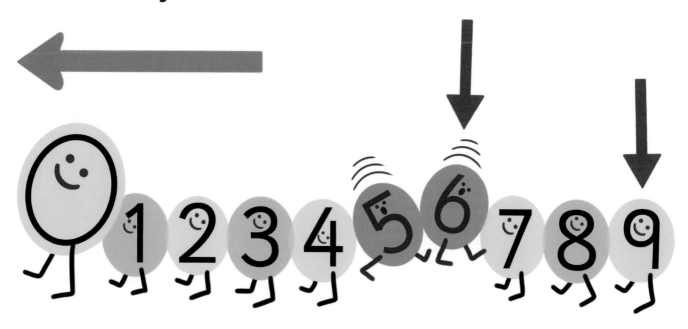

Find 6 and 9 on the caterpillar. Oh, 6 has a red face and is going in the wrong way. Five and six do not mix! But 9 is following 0.

I have another silly way to remember the difference between 6 and 9. I make them sit in a chair.

6 sits (**six sits**) in the chair.
It has a round bottom to make itself comfortable in the chair.

9 is too wobbly to sit in the chair. It doesn't have a round bottom!

Careful 9! Get off that chair or you'll hurt yourself.

Activity 16

Find all sixes and colour them in. Remember, **six sits**. Leave all nines as they are.

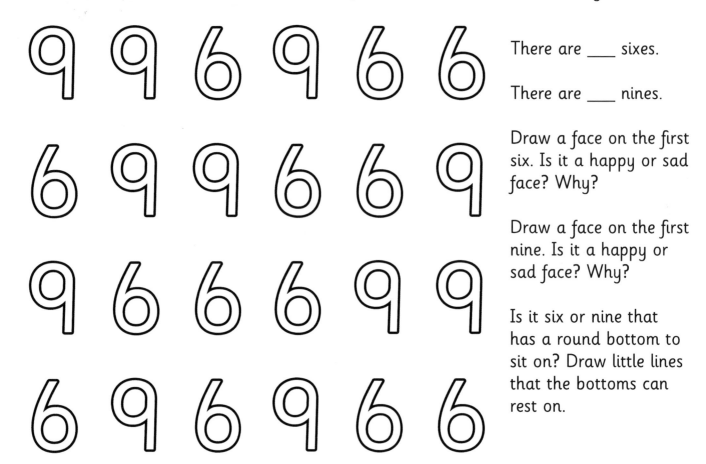

There are ___ sixes.

There are ___ nines.

Draw a face on the first six. Is it a happy or sad face? Why?

Draw a face on the first nine. Is it a happy or sad face? Why?

Is it six or nine that has a round bottom to sit on? Draw little lines that the bottoms can rest on.

Activity 17

Add the two numbers in each domino and write the sum in the bubble.

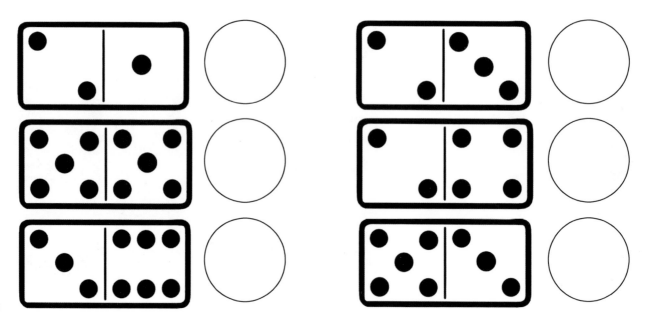

Activity 18

Time for skip counting! Can you work out the counting rule in each sequence?
Write down the missing numbers.

A. 0,   1,   2,   __,   4,   __,   __

B. 1,   __,   __,   7,   __,   11,   13

C. 8   __,   10,   11,   12,   __,   __

D. 15,   17,   __,   21,   __,   __,   __

E. __,   __,   __,   __,   7,   8,   __

F. __,   10,   __,   20,   __,   __,   35

G. 0,   4,   8,   __,   __,   20,   __

H. 3,   __,   23,   __,   __,   __,   63

I. __,   10,   __,   __,   25,   __,   35

J. __,   7,   __,   __,   10,   11,   __

K. 0,   __,   __,   __,   12,   15,   18

L. 1,   __,   11,   16,   21,   __,   __

M. __,   18,   27,   __,   45,   __,   __

11. Word and sentence lists

Read the words and sentences out loud to the child - one at a time and without showing the words to them.
Ask the child to find the tricky letters using the strategy they are currently learning, then to write down the word or full sentence. Encourage the child to practise writing at least 4-6 words and 1-2 sentences a day. Keep track of the child's progress and frequently go back to the same words and sentences to help the child 'over-learn' the letter shapes.

The lists below contain shorter and mostly phonologically regular words to avoid potential spelling problems while helping the child focus on the shape of the letters during writing.

b/d, p/g

pen, dog, gap, big, pad, bot, dig, peg, bid, dug, bet, pod, top, bee, dusk, post-man, beg, gut, bib, desk, pat, good, bin, top, pool, body, dust, pony, bank, gig, bud, bit, pug, ding dong, blob, gold, got, tip, bug, bed, pig, den, polka dot, boy, plug, bad, dam, park, dad, dim, boot, dip, bat, bold, bus, plan, dot, bend, pond, bun, pink, did, blot, had, bar, pin, hold, dash, fob, part, leg, pet, barn, cold, go, beef, pot, dark, bark, disk, bag, penny, banana, past, boom, pan, brush, plant, golf, gold.

s/z

zoom, sit, zest, sun, zoo, Sam, wiz, see, most, zigzag, set, slim, lazy, silk, zebra, sip, singer, zoo, small, snow, zigzag, sock, zip, soil, son, star, sky, zinc, set, still, maze, suntan, sum, zero, silly, Zac, sorry, spy, zing, starfish, snail, fizzy, snake, ski, zeal, silk, cozy, skip, sell, hazy, ask, quiz, size, zonk, sat, Tarzan, sister, snap.

b/d, p/g, s/z

bang, grasp, damp, sip, bishop, dusk, past, bold, dot, zap, bus, gust, best, zip, post, desk, sing, sad, zebra, dust, Zelda, buy, desk, buzz, spin, bet, bush, sport, boil, job, stop, soda, speed, bell, hub, bop, stand, step, bar, zombie, stop, zap, den, plus, beat, sugar, dozen, spider, sharp, bus, beef, soggy, gas, dam, Ziggy, sheep, bag, son, Iggy, bogus, spa, zoom, spark, mud, web, zone, boom, spoon, fed, blast, zoo, spot, belt, tub, club, both, better, number, spin, mud, kid, dog, hug, end, stamp, red, push, end, sleep, grass, glass, upset, along, bop, pea, sip.

p/q/g

peg, quick, goat, pick, quilt, gold, pit, quit, gig, pin, queen, golf, pack, quiz, guy, pun, quack, gas, pan, question, fig, past, queue, dig, pesto, quarry, mug, pink, quid, aqua, squid, equip, quake, quest, quote, equal, pug, mog, nag, veg, wag, jog, jug, mug, pod, hug, rug, gut, fog, pal, leg, ago, gran, glow, map, pop, grab, song, grow, lamp, long.

b/d, p/g

I bet you can't get to the bottom of the muddy pond to get the goldfish.
I plan to get there by bus - don't play the game until I bring bats and balls.
I dug in the garden to get the gold - I didn't do it to upset the bushes.
I had a banana on the bus but it wasn't good.
His dad's bank is so big it doesn't fit on the map.
Don't spend a penny on dinner. Dad will cook beef meatballs in gravy.

s/z

The fish and snails sizzled in a smoky pan.
Zac stopped at the zoo. A lazy zebra sat next to him in the sun.
Zoom in to see the zero on the sheet.
Zebras have silky, stripy skins.
I can't spot my sister in the maze with so many zigzags!
I like to slowly sip my zingy lemon drink. It's very fizzy.

p/q/g

The queen's quilt was quite long. It had patterns with grey polka dots.
Pandas are not as quick as pugs, never mind pumas.
When I hug gran, I get happy. She quietly gives me bags of sweets.
I had to quit my grand quest when the queen lost her crown in the game.

b/d, p/g, p/g, s/z

I did both the test and quiz in sixty seconds.
The hot day zapped my sporty spirit. I zonked out after a fizzy drink.
See the stars in the sky? They glow in the dark. Don't blink or they will pop.
The pop singer will play his gig in the park. There is a real buzz around the place.
Go to sleep, my little pet. Your legs will stop hurting.
Zac was upset after a black spider came down a spoon in his glass.

b/d (What are Bbs and Dds doing?)

Dad did the work.
Ben didn't do it.
Dan does a boring job.
Big Ben rings big bells.
Donald Duck can't read books.
Bob the Builder cooked the dish.

12. Key to activities

Activity 1 (across): doughnut, boat, bell, biscuit, book, duck, dinosaur, bubbles, bow, dog, boy, deer, blueberries, bucket, bag, bird, bicycle, baby.

Activity 2 (across): penny, goat, plug, gloves, garage, grater, pan, pond, plant, ghost, go/green, pony, pencil, pin, playground, golf, pot, glue.

Activity 3 (down): up, go, big, dog, Pat, bin, dig, bug, bib, Pig, bud, bad, peg, bed, gap, boy, bat, dad, bun, bus, bee, pen, pet, cold, pony, pink, bank, gold, barn, bald, plug, brush, penny, banana, postman.

Activity 4 (across): socks, zip, zigzag, snowflake, strawberry, sun, starfish, zebra, zoo, snail, sandwich.

Activity 5
Hello Mr Zombie,
You are not scary. You are silly! Zombies don't like the sun. They sleep during the day. It's almost dusk, past your bedtime. Zombies don't stay in a zoo with zebras and snakes, and they are not scared of spiders! They don't sing songs or ride on zip wires. Please stop being a silly zombie. Stanley is a wizard and he can help zap your silly bug. We can then be best friends again.
Hugs,
Sammy x

Activity 7 (across): door, ballerina, dice, drum, balloon, disc, block/brick, butterfly, bin, bee, ball, bib, dancing, bus.

Activity 10 (across): panda, digger, broccoli, queen, gate, pie, peacock, bear, quiet, pencil, quilt, donkey, question, bunny, gorilla, baker, penguin, dragon, bat, peas, dolphin, bread, guitar, grasshopper, bud, quick.

Activity 12
a b c d e f g h i j k l m n o p q r s t u v w x y z

Activity 16
There are 13 sixes.
There are 11 nines.

Activity 17
2 + 1 = 3	2 + 3 = 5
5 + 5 = 10	2 + 4 = 6
3 + 6 = 9	5 + 3 = 8

Activity 18
A.   0, 1, 2, 3, 4, 5, 6
B.   1, 3, 5, 7, 9, 11, 13
C.   8, 9, 10, 11, 12, 13, 14
D.   15, 17, 19, 21, 23, 25, 27
E.   3, 4, 5, 6, 7, 8, 9
F.   5, 10, 15, 20, 25, 30, 35
G.   0, 4, 8, 12, 16, 20, 24
H.   3, 13, 23, 33, 43, 53, 63
I.   5, 10, 15, 20, 25, 30, 35
J.   6, 7, 8, 9, 10, 11, 12
K.   0, 3, 6, 9, 12, 15, 18
L.   1, 6, 11, 16, 21, 26, 31
M.   9, 18, 27, 36, 45, 54, 63

Printed by Amazon Italia Logistica S.r.l.
Torrazza Piemonte (TO), Italy

32857129R00020